BUSES ON THE WESTERN ISLES

RICHARD WALTER

Front cover: New to Lochs Motor Transport in 2020 was this very smart-looking MCV eVoRa bodied Volvo B8RLE SJ20 KNL. The eVoRa is the successor to the MCV Evolution and is also available on the Volvo B5LH chassis.

Back cover: A line-up at the council depot at Marybank of some of the Bus Na Comhairle BMC 1100FEs used for local school contracts until 2019.

First published 2021

Amberley Publishing
The Hill, Stroud
Gloucestershire, GL5 4EP

www.amberley-books.com

Copyright © Richard Walter, 2021

The right of Richard Walter to be identified as the Author of this work has been asserted in accordance with the Copyrights, Designs and Patents Act 1988.

ISBN 978 1 3981 0454 9 (print)
ISBN 978 1 3981 0455 6 (ebook)

All rights reserved. No part of this book may be reprinted or reproduced or utilised in any form or by any electronic, mechanical or other means, now known or hereafter invented, including photocopying and recording, or in any information storage or retrieval system, without the permission in writing from the Publishers.

British Library Cataloguing in Publication Data.
A catalogue record for this book is available from the British Library.

Origination by Amberley Publishing.
Printed in the UK.

Appointed GPSR EU Representative: Easy Access System Europe Oü, 16879218
Address: Mustamäe tee 50, 10621, Tallinn, Estonia
Contact Details: gpsr.requests@easproject.com, +358 40 500 3575

Contents

Introduction	4
Bus Na Comhairle	6
Classique Tours	24
Galson Motors	25
Hebridean Transport	38
Hebridean Coaches, South Uist	51
Lochs Motor Transport	52
MacDonald Coaches	75
Maclennan Coaches	78
South Harris Coaches	87
Peter Maclennan	88
Other Operators	91
Visiting Vehicles to the Western Isles	94
Preserved Buses on the Western Isles	96

Introduction

To those of you who have a copy of the excellent 2014 Amberley Publishing book *Buses of Skye and the Western Isles* by John Sinclair, you will have appreciated the interesting history of bus services there in the 1960s and 1970s. In this book, I have illustrated some of the developments between 2010 and 2020 – a period that saw significant changes in vehicle types and the services provided. I have tried to illustrate how the providers of buses and coaches on the Western Isles have had to adapt to new ways or working to meet changing demands. The period between the two books is a story of its own in which all sorts of interesting vehicles (many being former Scottish Bus Group buses) were in service. I hope to cover it in a future book.

In the beautiful Outer Hebrides, the islands of Lewis and Harris offer challenges faced by few other areas in the UK. Weather can change rapidly from sunny to stormy. Buses must often cope with the worst of conditions and there are many single-track roads where great care has to be taken to avoid falling into ditches.

Travelling by bus in the Outer Hebrides is inexpensive, but some services do not operate every day and certain sections on some routes are covered on a request-only basis.

The local council, Comhairle nan Eilean Siar, requires companies to tender for bus services on the islands on a regular basis, and those who tender have to be aware of the requirements for low-floor vehicles despite the unpredictable terrain.

As tourism has increased on the island, visitors' expectations of quality and reliability have grown. Also key to the economy of the islands has been the rise in visits by cruise ships which berth off Stornoway and convey passengers to the shore for short tours. The local operators take a share in providing coach transport, and after years of sourcing older second-hand vehicles they have now heavily invested in modern fleets. The passengers arriving off the ships understandably expect coaches to feature comfortable seats, air conditioning, Wi-Fi and charging ports for their mobile phones and tablets. Vehicles acquired over recent years have had to include these necessities along with proper ticket machines and contactless payment options on service buses.

During 2019, the council suggested a number of options to save £1.67 million out of its overall £6.6 million transport services budget, of which school and public bus services made up the vast bulk of running costs. With the prospect of reduced services to rural villages, locals were understandably concerned. Not only were there changes to timetables, but some services moved to other operators. One of the biggest changes was the tender for the Stornoway to Ness service being awarded to Lochs Motor Transport after Galson Motors had provided the route for over forty years.

In 2000, a small group of locals formed to safeguard the transport heritage of the Western Isles and preserve the oral, written and photographic history of motorised transport within the islands. The Western Isles Transport Preservation Group (WITPG), as it is known, has acquired an old fish farm processing plant which is being used as a base for their operations and a future museum site for which they are trying to generate funding. Full details of the work of the WITPG can be found at http://www.witpg.org.uk.

The tragic arrival of the coronavirus epidemic in 2020 has led to a very uncertain future for the bus and coach industry. The loss of visiting cruise ships and tourists, the cancellation of the annual Heb Celt Music Festival and the temporary suspension of school services were severe blows to operators on the Western Isles. These troubled months are reflected in some of the photos featured. However, there is a great sense of optimism that 2021 will be a much better year, and preparations are in place to ensure that the operators are up and running to meet the requirements of visitors.

My grateful thanks go to John Sinclair for inspiring the book, Roddy Macdonald of Lochs Motor Transport for all his help and advice over the years and to Alistair Train and John MacDonald for their photographic contributions. I would especially like to thank local experts Steven Macaskill and Donald Macarthur for providing detailed information and much-appreciated assistance in preparation of the book together with some of their excellent photos. They are credited for their work. The uncredited pictures were taken by me. Do go and pay the islands a visit if you have never been. Along with the delights of the islands, be sure to take some time to observe the interesting buses and coaches.

Richard Walter
September 2020

Lochs Motor Transport Jonkheere SD15 UWL completing the afternoon school run coming out of the village of Portvoller in the Point area of Lewis. (Donald Macarthur)

Bus Na Comhairle

New to First Huddersfield was BMC 1100FE B133 (YJ05 PUX), which joined the council specifically for school contracts. It is seen on the pits at the council's Marybank depot, which houses all types of vehicles operated including cleansing services stock.

For the annual Lewis Carnival procession in July 2019, BMC 1100FE B133 (YJ05 PUX) became the Boris's Love Island on Lewis bus with a number of Boris Johnson lookalikes on board and cycling beside the vehicle. Thousands of spectators lined the streets of Stornoway to watch the procession wind its way from Willowglen to Perceval Square. (Steven Macaskill)

Seen in the very picturesque setting of Portnaguran with an Optare Solo in the background is another view of BMC 1100FE B133 (YJ05 PUX). (Donald Macarthur)

BMC 1100FE B135 (YJ05 KOW) was pictured at the back of the council depot at Marybank and shows the additional maroon swoops carried by this vehicle from its previous ownership with First Huddersfield where it was numbered 68541.

Showing the spectacular backdrop of New Tolsta at the end of the afternoon school run is BMC 1100FE B143 (BX06 OCZ). (Donald Macarthur)

A fine line-up at the ferry terminal in Stornoway of all the BMC 1100FEs following their withdrawal from service and about to leave the islands in 2019. (Donald Macarthur)

Dennis Javelin B126 (R917 HTW), previously with the Lochs Motor Transport fleet, sits in Marybank depot in the attractive yellow and white livery. In its latter days it appeared primarily on school contracts but was also seen on service work, often stepping in for Plaxton Centro bodied VDL SB200 B128 (YN07 KGU).

Dennis Javelin B119 (M7 SEL), in the more traditional council livery of all white with yellow striping, was photographed after withdrawal from service where it remained at Marybank depot for some time before being scrapped.

Bought as new, Plaxton Centro bodied VDL SB200 B128 (YN07 KGU) represented the first low-floor vehicle on the islands and initially appeared in this rather sombre dark green and white livery.

Another photo of Plaxton Centro bodied VDL SB200 B128 (YN07 KGU) being used as a shuttle bus into Stornoway during one of the popular annual motor shows held by the Western Isles Preservation Group at the Tong Showground.

The green was eventually replaced with council yellow on Plaxton Centro bodied VDL SB200 B128 (YN07 KGU), seen here arriving in Stornoway on service W5 from Tolsta.

A decision was taken in December 2019 to remove Plaxton Centro bodied VDL SB200 B128 (YN07 KGU) from service following a number of engine transmission and electrical system faults being detected. The bus is leaving Stornoway bus station bound for Tolsta on the W5 shortly before its withdrawal from service.

Up until 2014, Bus Na Comhairle operated various school contracts in Uist and Benbecula. This is the Comhairle's Market Stance depot in Benbecula with the three Uist-based coaches photographed. Caetano bodied Dennis Javelin B127 (P175 ANR) is seen here with Plaxton Prima bodied Dennis Javelin B114 (R777 GSM) and similar B118 (M6 SEL) in the background. (Donald Macarthur)

Pictured at Marybank depot is Plaxton Beaver 2 bodied Mercedes-Benz O814D KF52 TZO, which was originally from Tally Ho of Kingsbridge. It was loaned from Dawson Rentals on two separate occasions.

Another Plaxton Beaver 2 bodied Mercedes-Benz O814D was YN04 HJF, seen resting between duties in Stornoway bus station. Note the blinds which contained destinations in English and Gaelic – the latter in a very traditional stylised font.

Arriving at the turning point at Swordale in Point is Plaxton Beaver 2 bodied Mercedes-Benz O814D YN54 XYK showing a more basic screen.

Nicknamed 'The Ambulance Bus' by the drivers because of the style of the welfare rear doors was unique Plaxton Beaver 2 bodied Mercedes-Benz Vario X174 BNH. The distinctive clock tower of Stornoway Town Hall is in the background.

Only with the council for a short time was Plaxton Beaver 2 bodied Mercedes-Benz Vario PF51 KHB, originally new to Shuttle Buses of Kilwinning. (Donald Macarthur)

New in April 2011 and seen on delivery coming off the Caledonian MacBrayne ferry MV *Isle of Lewis* from Ullapool is Plaxton Beaver 3 bodied Mercedes-Benz O813D YX11 CUK. The bus received the fleet number B140 and the whole batch featured digital screens. It was sold along with the rest of the batch to Docherty's of Auchterarder. (Donald Macarthur)

Another of the batch of Plaxton Beaver 3 bodied Mercedes-Benz Varios was B142 (YX11 CUO), seen here reversing into the small turning circle at the edge of Point in Swordale.

Plaxton Beaver 3 bodied Mercedes-Benz Vario B138 (YX11 CUG) also pictured in Point. A service to Bayble serves the village of Swordale at certain times of the day – some journeys are by passenger request only.

Sunrise and sunset on the Western Isles can be a truly beautiful time rivalling some of the best views from hot climates. This spectacular shot of Optare Solo SR B150 (YJ14 BDU) was taken at Portnaguran Pier. (Donald Macarthur)

Optare Solo SR B150 (YJ14 BDU) passes by one of the many wind farm turbines on Lewis. This particular turbine is in Tolsta and is operated by Tolsta Power Ltd, a trading subsidy of Tolsta Community Development Limited (TCDL). Tolsta Power Ltd gift aids part of the profit from the turbine back to TCDL once all the operating costs, operational insurance, bank loans and VAT have been paid. This money benefits the Tolsta community directly with every household receiving some sort of benefit from it. (Steven Macaskill)

Optare Solo SR B152 (YJ14 BDX) is seen on the Eye Peninsula driving up from Tiumpan Head Lighthouse. (Steven Macaskill)

Passing through Aignish and about to cross the Braigh (a causeway) into Stornoway is Optare Solo SR B152 (YJ14 BDX). During severe stormy weather, when huge waves can sweep dangerously over the main road, the Braigh is often closed to traffic, isolating all the villages on that side of the island from Stornoway itself.

Optare Solo SR B152 (YJ14 BDX) is swamped by the impressive An Lanntair arts centre building, which is also home to the one and only permanent cinema on Lewis. The bus station is conveniently situated across the road.

There are many single-track roads on the islands with suitable passing places for vehicles to use. Optare Solo SR B153 (YJ14 BDY) negotiates a narrow road in Portvoller. (Donald Macarthur)

It's carnival time on Lewis, as indicated by the flags. Optare Solo SR B153 (YJ14 BDY) drives past Stornoway Harbour on a sunny summer's day.

Seen heading into Stornoway is Optare Solo SR B156 (YJ67 GCO), which was bought from Galson Motors in January 2020 (see page 30).

Having turned at the foot of the village, similar Optare Solo SR B154 (YJ14 BDZ) was pictured heading back out of Swordale.

Another short-term visitor to the fleet was Plaxton Centro bodied VDL SB200 B147 (YJ58 FFD) pictured at Portnaguran Pier. It was originally with Reays Coaches of Wigton. (Donald Macarthur)

On loan to the council was Wright Streetlite MX61 BBV, previously with Astons Coaches, heading along South Beach with a driver getting familiar with the new type of vehicle. (Donald Macarthur)

The council borrowed several vehicles whilst awaiting its new batch of vehicles in 2014. Optare Solo B149 (YJ59 NNO), heading a number of Plaxton Beaver 3s, was leased to Arriva from Dawson Rentals and was previously with Heyfordian of Bicester. (Donald Macarthur)

Optare Solo B148 (MX09 AOU), photographed at Stornoway bus station, was another short-term loaned vehicle, originally belonging to Sanders and Jackson of Silsden. (Donald Macarthur)

Seen between runs in the bus station in Stornoway is the council's largest bus at the time of writing. B155 is an ADL bodied Enviro200 MK63 XAA, although it does not have a fleet number applied.

ADL bodied Enviro200 B155 (MK63 XAA) on the W5 showing in the screen that it is on one of the journeys that calls at Stornoway airport.

Classique Tours

Classique Tours operated a working museum of classic British coaches ranging from 1949 to the present day throughout parts of Scotland. They were all restored to the very high standards required by the Department of Transport. Plaxton bodied Leyland Leopard PSU3BR/4R 'Brighton Belle' (SRC 45L) started its life with Southdown Motor Services. Sadly their Outer Hebrides tours did not last long. It was pictured in Harris after the tours had ceased. (Alistair Train)

Very distinctive 1950 Harrington bodied Leyland Tiger PS2 'Janice' (GDM 494) is also seen in Harris following its use on the Classique Tours. All the coaches in the fleet had fewer than the maximum number of seats, allowing extra legroom and added luxury in which to enjoy the fine scenic views of Scotland.

Galson Motors

At Galson Motors garage out at Lower Barvas is Volvo JIL 3713, which latterly served with Maclennan of Grosebay. The company was formed in 1948 from four separate independent bus owners in the Borve and Shader areas on the west side of Lewis.

Bound for Ness is Plaxton Premiere bodied Volvo B10M L345 ERU, which previously operated with Excelsior and Blackburn Transport.

Parked by Tesco near the ferry terminal in Stornoway is Van Hool Alizee bodied Volvo B10M-62 M658 ROS, which was new to Hutchison's of Overtown in 1995. It subsequently passed to Whitestar Coaches of Neilston and then to Stuart's Coaches of Carluke.

Vehicles between journeys used to park in the industrial estates within Stornoway centre. Bought from Harris Coaches of Tarbert, Plaxton bodied Volvo B10M V58 KWO was new to Bebb Travel in Wales.

Another photo of Plaxton bodied Volvo B10M V58 KWO heading into Stornoway in service from Ness.

Plaxton Beaver 2 bodied Mercedes-Benz Vario O814D SK02 NYU at the company's garage at Lower Barvas.

Also seen at Lower Barvas is Plaxton Cheetah bodied Mercedes-Benz O813D SF04 HXP, which was bought new by MacDonald Coaches of Balallan.

In more recent years, Galson Motors have adopted a more basic all-white livery as shown by Mercedes-Benz T782 RSF at the garage.

Plaxton Beaver 2 Mercedes-Benz O813D SJ08 WAF and similar SC58 OHB at Lower Barvas.

Galson Motors operated a number of smaller buses such as this Plaxton Beaver 2 bodied Mercedes-Benz O813D SC58 OHB.

Optare Solo YJ10 OAD was bought from Kineil Coaches of Fraserburgh in April 2016 and was loaned to Bus Na Comhairle on multiple occasions. Pictured here on an early evening, it is screened up for the Nicolson Institute secondary school in Stornoway. The bus passed to Ace Mini Coaches in late 2019 and was re-registered as L21 AMC. (Donald Macarthur)

In February 2018, Optare Solo SR YJ67 GCO was acquired and primarily used on evening services. In January 2020 it passed to Bus Na Comhairle (see page 20).

Ford Transit bodied Ford FJ14 UTX was bought new in April 2014. (Steven Macaskill)

Ford Transit bodied Ford SN18 WFC, new to the company in March 2019, and similar GA15 ONS, new in April 2015. (Steven Macaskill)

Looking very smart is Van Hool Alizee T9 Volvo B12B NE52 STY approaching Stornoway bus station. This vehicle was new to Marbill Travel as SF03 AWC.

Van Hool Alizee T9 Volvo B12B NE52 STY in very different weather conditions braving heavy snowfall. (Donald Macarthur)

Van Hool Alizee bodied Volvo B10B SF03 AWC pictured before it received the registration mark of NE52 STY.

Van Hool Alizee bodied Volvo B10M-62 JSV 486 (ex S768 OTR) started life with Galvin, Dunmanway, County Cork registered as 99-C-5098. It also operated with Hamish Gordon, Leslie, Fife.

Formerly with Marbill Travel of Beith is Van Hool bodied Volvo Y991 TSD. This coach passed to MacPhail of Salsburgh as N80 JHM.

YJ03 VMR – a Plaxton Paragon bodied Volvo B12M new to Wallace Arnold is seen at Stornoway bus station.

Passing the main shops in Stornoway is Van Hool bodied Volvo B12M WA54 HXV, new to Chalfont, Southall in October 2004, passing to Lochs Motor Transport in June 2012 for their Inverness to Ullapool service. It then moved to Galson Motors in February 2014. It has since been acquired by Miller of Airdrie in late 2019.

Another view of Van Hool bodied Volvo B12M WA54 HXV.

Van Hool Alizee bodied Volvo B12B SK05 SOU was new to Southern Coaches of Barrhead in June 2005 and purchased by Galson Motors in April 2016. (Steven Macaskill)

Jonkheere SHV bodied Volvo B12B FJ58 LSK was purchased in April 2016 having been T66 MOS with Macleans of Stranraer. It was new to AAA Coaches of Edinburgh in November 2008.

Plaxton Panther bodied Volvo B9R YJ14 NLK was new to Lochs Motor Transport in July 2014 and passed to Galson Motors in July 2018. It is seen here reversing out of the Lochs Motor Transport garage at Cameron Terrace after receiving Galson Motors logos.

Another shot of Plaxton Panther bodied Volvo B9R YJ14 NLK prior to being delivered to Galson Motors.

Hebridean Transport

Hebridean Transport is based at the Parkend Industrial Estate in Sandwick near Stornoway. Plaxton Premiere 320 bodied Dennis Javelin N406 SPC was one of several vehicles acquired from Epsom Coaches and which ran in their former operator's livery whilst with Hebridean Transport. The vehicle passes Stornoway Town Hall on its long journey to Leverburgh in Harris.

Plaxton Premiere 320 bodied Dennis Javelin N406 SPC again. It was photographed at the ferry terminal at Tarbert in Harris.

About to set out from Leverburgh for Stornoway is Plaxton Premiere 320 bodied Dennis Javelin N479 VPA.

Plaxton Premiere 320 bodied Dennis Javelin P707 DPA takes a rest outside Tesco in Stornoway before it heads back to Harris.

Plaxton Premiere 320 bodied Dennis Javelin P707 DPA in typical scenery between Lewis and Harris. The roads are mostly single carriageways now, but for many years there were large stretches of single-track road along the way. There are still many single-track roads in Lewis and Harris. Most villages have single-track roads, as do parts of Uig and most of the area south of Tarbert in Harris.

Despite being a small bus, Plaxton Cheetah bodied Mercedes-Benz O814D FNZ 5834, which was new to Chambers, Moneymore in 2004, was a regular performer of the Stornoway to Leverburgh service. Seen here as it arrives in Stornoway.

YN04 HJX was a similar Plaxton Cheetah bodied Mercedes-Benz O814D from Bibby of Ingleton acquired in 2009. Loaded up with passengers, it is ready for the return trip to Tarbert and Leverburgh in 2010.

A year later in 2011, and looking like it has had some accident repairs, Plaxton Cheetah bodied Mercedes-Benz O814D YN04 HJX leaves the bus station in Stornoway.

A smaller bus in the fleet was Ford Minibus YL55 HWY, pictured here whilst in Stornoway. The bus was used on the Grimshader Feeder for the short time it ran.

Plaxton Panther bodied Volvo B10M W209 EAG came from Redline Motor Coaches of Great Yarmouth. The coach is dropping off passengers at the stop close to the busy Cromwell Street in the centre of Stornoway.

Plaxton Premier bodied Volvo B10M T504 EUB was new to Wallace Arnold in March 1999. It passed to Maclennan Coaches in March 2009 and then to Hebridean Transport in March 2014 remaining in Maclennan's grey livery.

With the Caledonian MacBrayne ferry MV *Hebrides* in the background, Plaxton Premiere bodied Volvo B10M T504 EUB is seen on the way to Sir E Scott school in Tarbert. (Donald Macarthur)

MV64 ZWA is one of two Ford Transit bodied Fords bought as new in September 2014. The other one is MC64 ZVY.

Ford Transit MV64 ZWA is a very versatile bus with disabled access. The photo shows it at Leverburgh ferry terminal about to depart for Stornoway.

Plaxton Profile bodied Volvo B7R HC04 AAA was acquired in October 2014 having been with Henry Cooper, Newcastle and P&O Lloyd, North Wales. It passes Stornoway Town Hall on a bright and sunny afternoon, showing off the most recent cream livery adopted by the company.

Fleet expansion in 2019 saw the arrival of a number of Irizar i6 bodied Scania K340IB4s. YP12 NUJ was new to Redwing Reliance, London and purchased from Maclennan Coaches in October 2019.

Awaiting passengers in Stornoway bus station is Plaxton Profile bodied Volvo B7R WM03 BYD, which was new to First Wessex.

Plaxton Profile bodied Volvo B7R SW59 MLE was acquired in August 2016, having started life with Johnson Transport of Shetland as J600 JFJ.

Parking up at Tarbert ferry terminal is Irizar Century bodied Scania K340EB4 YN07 EXS, which was new to Sunrise Direct, Fencabs in May 2007 and purchased in April 2016.

Another photo of Irizar Century bodied Scania K340EB4 YN07 EXS in Tarbert.

Irizar Century bodied Scania K340EB4 YN07 EXS heading through Stornoway on a school contract.

Plaxton Profile bodied Volvo B7R SW59 MLE in the town of Stornoway.

EVM Avantgarde bodied Mercedes-Benz 516 Cdi RX70 RZU is used on the westside circular service during off-peak times when a coach is not necessary. It was pictured operating the lunchtime run to Shawbost. (Donald Macarthur)

Irizar i6 bodied Scania K340IB4 HB12 HEB, which was new to Terravision, London as YT12 YUA in April 2012 and acquired in July 2017.

Irizar i6 bodied Scania K340IB4 AB12 HEB with the impressive Stornoway Town Hall in the background.

Irizar i6 bodied Scania K340IB4s AB12 HEB rests between journeys showing how well the company livery suits this style of coach.

Hebridean Coaches, South Uist

Hebridean Coaches were based at Howmore on South Uist. The company was family run for over seventy years and operated services from Eriskay in the south to Lochmaddy in North Uist. Pictured is Plaxton Cheetah bodied Mercedes-Benz O814 DHIG 2462. (Donald Macarthur)

Plaxton Premiere 320 bodied Dennis Javelin HIG 2461. The company's workshop facilities, where cars and heavy goods vehicles were repaired, were available to the public. (Donald Macarthur)

Lochs Motor Transport

Established in 1947, the company is based in Leurbost and has over fifty years of driving experience all over the north of Scotland. In the photo is Plaxton Beaver 2 bodied Mercedes-Benz O813D YN09 KHL, which latterly served with Felix of Sudbury. It is seen on the W8 service to Ranish, which Lochs Motor Transport took over again in 2009 having been operated by Hebridean Transport for ten years.

Another shot of Plaxton Beaver 2 bodied Mercedes-Benz O813D YN09 KHL on Matheson Road making its way to Stornoway bus station.

Wintry conditions in 2010 for Plaxton Beaver 2 bodied Mercedes-Benz O813D YN09 KHL, seen loading in Leurbost. (John MacDonald)

The replacement for the Plaxton Beaver came in the form of ADL Enviro200 YX60 DXR with a greater seating capacity for service work. The vehicle is now fleet number 510 with Centrebus in Northampton.

ADL Enviro200 YX60 DXR in the centre of Stornoway on its way to the bus station.

A replacement ADL Enviro200 in 2014 was similar YX64 VPG pictured leaving Stornoway for Ranish.

The third ADL Enviro200 owned by Lochs Motor Transport was YX17 NRL, bought new in July 2017 and subsequently sold in May 2020 to J & D Halcrow in Shetland. The photograph shows the vehicle arriving on the island by Caledonian MacBrayne ferry MV *Loch Seaforth* – the largest vessel in service.

Another view coming off the ferry of ADL Enviro200 YX17 NRL already wearing the smart company livery and fleet names.

ADL Enviro200 YX17 NRL in service en route to Ranish passing Stornoway Town Hall.

Seen approaching Cameron Terrace is ADL Enviro200 YX17 NRL showing the direction signs for the West Side tourist attractions and various other parts of the islands. (Steven Macaskill)

New to Lochs Motor Transport in 2020 was this very smart-looking MCV eVoRa bodied Volvo B8RLE SJ20 KNL, which replaced the 17 plate Enviro200. The eVoRa is the successor to the MCV Evolution and is also available on the Volvo B5LH chassis. It was introduced in 2018.

Another view of MCV eVoRa bodied Volvo B8RLE SJ20 KNL leaving Sgoil Nan Loch (Lochs School) in Leurbost on a rather wet and miserable day.

Setting the trends for passenger comfort on the islands is MCV eVoRa bodied Volvo B8RLE SJ20 KNL, seen in Stornoway town centre.

Lochs have been very happy with the performance of MCV eVoRa bodied Volvo B8RLE SJ20 KNL since its entry into service in June 2020.

Seen at the South Lochs turn at Balallan is Plaxton Prima bodied Dennis Javelin R917 HTW, which was new to Biss Brothers, Stansted in May 1998. It subsequently passed to Bus Na Comhairle in March 2007.

Seen at the garage in an incomplete livery was short-term-owned Plaxton Paragon bodied Volvo B10M-62 Y738 HWT, which now belongs to 1st Call Travel, Merthyr Tydfil in Wales.

Leaving Stornoway ferry terminal with cruise ship passengers is Plaxton Paragon bodied Volvo B10M-62 Y504 TGJ, which originally came from Express Motors in North Wales.

Parked on pier number 3 in Stornoway is Plaxton Volvo B12M YN03 WXU picking up passengers from a cruise ship which is out of shot. The Caledonian MacBrayne ferry MV *Isle of Lewis* can be seen behind the coaches. The vehicle was later sold to Irving of Dalston.

Plaxton Paragon Panther bodied Volvo B9R YU05 VFL on cruise ship duties at Stornoway ferry terminal.

Purchased as new in October 2011, and at the time of writing the oldest coach in the fleet, is Plaxton Panther bodied Volvo B9R SY61 AUL, which was used briefly on the Inverness to Ullapool service in 2012. It has recently been made PSVAR compliant with a wheelchair lift and LED destination screens being added.

New to Lochs Motor Transport was Plaxton Panther 2 bodied Volvo B9R YN12 BXL, full of visitors to the islands away for a short tour.

Plaxton Elite bodied Volvo B9R YY14 NLN was sold to Shiel Buses of Acharacle in 2017 and painted yellow and blue for Scottish Citylink services.

Two new vehicles were acquired in 2014, one of them being Plaxton Panther bodied Volvo B9R YY14 NLK. Whilst the 64 plate Enviro200 was away for replacement by the 17 plate one, this vehicle was used on the W8 Ranish service. The picture shows it passing the popular Caladh Inn (previously the Seaforth Hotel) in Stornoway.

Plaxton Panther bodied Volvo B9R YY14 NLK again providing passengers with some luxury not usually to be found on the Stornoway to Ranish bus service. It is seen by the Town Hall in Stornoway.

Jonkheere SHV bodied Volvo B11R SD15 UWL with onboard toilet was bought new in April 2015. It awaits cruise ship passengers at the Stornoway ferry terminal with guides connecting other travellers with their particular coach for a short trip round the islands.

Jonkheere SHV bodied Volvo B11R SD15 UWL is seen at the far end of the village of Swordale on an afternoon school run.

Plaxton Leopard Volvo B8R YX66 WMZ, bought new in October 2016, pictured at the Lochs garage. The company's relationship with Plaxton goes back many years with their vehicles dominating the fleet.

Plaxton Leopard Volvo B8R YX66 WMZ on a school contract to Lower Bayble. Lochs Motor Transport attempts to provide stylish, high-quality vehicles that consistently perform well on the islands' often treacherous roads while offering both driver and passenger appeal.

Jonkheere SHV bodied Volvo B11R SF17 VMR shortly after delivery on a sunny morning at Lochs' depot.

In contrast to the Plaxton vehicles, Jonkheere SHV bodied Volvo B11R SF17 VMR was bought new in April 2017. It has a very different look to it. Undertaking an excursion for cruise ship passengers, it is seen leaving Stornoway ferry terminal.

Plaxton Elite bodied Volvo B11R YX18 LHK was bought new in March 2018. All the features included are expected of a modern coach, among them automatic dimming lights in the saloon, gangway LED lighting, recliner seats with three-point safety belts, radio and DVD, PA system, eight-camera CCTV, GPS tracking and alloy wheels.

Another garage photo of Plaxton Elite bodied Volvo B11R YX18 LHK when newly acquired.

Plaxton Panther bodied Volvo B11R YX68 UAG providing the W8 Ranish service, which covers numerous pick-up points in the north of the island. (Donald Macarthur)

A garage view of Plaxton Panther bodied Volvo B11R YX68 UAG, which features a DDA compliant wheelchair lift, was bought new in December 2018. Like other vehicles in the fleet it was bought for service routes, school contracts, tours (including the excursions provided for cruise ship passengers) and private hires.

In April 2018, Lochs Motor Transport acquired ex-Southern Coaches of Barrhead Plaxton Panther bodied Volvo B9R OO3 SOU. It remained in the livery of Southern Coaches for its short stay in Lewis, with Lochs fleet names being applied. The vehicle left the fleet in December of the same year.

Trialled for short while was Plaxton Cheetah XL bodied Mercedes-Benz FJ18 OFA. Only about 100 of this type were built. (Donald Macarthur)

Photographed passing the garage at Leurbost on a school contract is Unvi bodied Mercedes 1524L PO14 ATF, which was new to Coastal Coaches in Warton (North Lancashire) in April 2014 and purchased by Lochs in March 2019.

Also performing a school contract is Sunsundegui Sideral bodied Volvo B7R BC64 NBC (new to Bharat, Southall in September 2014 and ex-Doigs of Glasgow in October 2019, which was on loan from Volvo during 2020.

Following the successful bid for services during in 2019, Lochs Motor Transport needed to quickly expand its fleet. Pictured on a bright but wet day is Caetano Levante bodied Volvo B9R FJ13 EBZ, new to Kings Ferry in Gillingham, Kent in May 2013 and purchased by Lochs in September 2019. (Donald Macarthur)

Arriving at Stornoway bus station is Caetano Levante bodied Volvo B9R FJ13 EBZ.

Irizar i6 bodied Scania K360IB4s YP12 NUW and YP12 NUX were both new to Redwing Reliance in London in June 2012 and purchased by Lochs in September 2019. YP12 NUW, pictured here, spent some time with Reays in Wigton where it was registered as 7 TXN.

Plaxton Leopard bodied Volvo B9R YX15 OVD was new to Horseman, Reading in March 2015 and purchased by Lochs in October 2019. Its seating has been increased from C59F to C72F. Here it is being reversed out of the maintenance shed in a torrential downpour. The weather on the Isles is very unpredictable and often changes several times in a short period.

New to Glenton Tours/Parks of Hamilton and later with Pulham, Bourton-on-the-Water is Plaxton Elite bodied Volvo B9R SN15 KMM (also registered as KSK 950) just after being acquired by Lochs in August 2020 and awaiting the application of vinyls. It is pictured operating between Stornoway and Tarbert.

Purchased at the same time is similar Plaxton Elite bodied Volvo B9R SC15 ZNK (LSK 514) – also new to Parks of Hamilton and ex-Acklams, Beverley – heading through Leurbost en route to Stornoway in a heavy rain shower.

YO16 JHJ is one of two Ford Transit bodied Fords previously with a school in the Glasgow area. The other one is HN16 CMO. Both were acquired in September 2019. (Steven Macaskill)

Ford Transit bodied Ford YJ69 VLP was one of two similar vehicles bought as new in October 2019. The other vehicle is YJ69 VLR. (Donald Macarthur)

MacDonald Coaches

MacDonald Coaches operate from Balallan in South Lochs. Ford Transit bodied Ford CV62 VFO was bought new in January 2013. It was photographed at the Leurbost garage of Lochs Motor Transport where the company vehicles go to for maintenance.

An older style of livery applied to Ford Transit bodied Ford SG62 EFZ which was formally with Peter Maclennan.

Jonkheere Mistral bodied Volvo B12B WA04 YZR in the distinctive livery for MacDonald Coaches.

Plaxton Elite bodied Volvo B9R YN10 EOT (ex-Howard Snaith, Otterburn in March 2018) parked in Bayble.

Lit up by the morning sun is Jonkheere SHV bodied Volvo B9R SJ15 PVA, which was bought new in May 2015.

Sunsundegui Sideral bodied Volvo B7 BU14 EHD passing the depot of Lochs Motor Transport en route to the village of Keose on the afternoon school run from Sgoil Nan Loch (Lochs School). (Donald Macarthur)

Maclennan Coaches

Based in premises in Incalete Road, Stornoway, Maclennan Coaches operate a wide variety of small and larger coaches. Seen on the outskirts of Stornoway is Plaxton Premiere bodied Volvo B10M T527 EUB (GIB 976), which was purchased from Weardale Motor Services in Durham.

The unique and attractive style of bodywork on Plaxton Paragon Volvo B10M-62 GX51 CFF.

Plaxton Premiere bodied Volvo B10M-62 T599 BRG, later transferred to Hebridean Transport.

Near the Callanish Visitor Centre is Plaxton Profile bodied Dennis Javelin AL03 ASH, which was new to Ashford Luxury, Bedfont in June 2003 and purchased by Maclennan Coaches in May 2011. The visitor centre is beside the world-famous Callanish standing stones – one of Scotland's most magnificent and best-preserved Neolithic monuments. (Donald Macarthur)

Returning cruise ship passengers to Stornoway is Jonkheere SHV bodied Volvo B12M PN08 KWX, which was bought in June 2015 from Travellers Choice of Carnforth where it was registered 4 ORX.

On service work into Stornoway is Van Hool Alizee bodied Scania K114 SX04 XAC, which was bought in April 2014. Formerly ex-Eirebus, Dublin, where it was registered 04-D-35350.

Entering Stornoway bus station is Van Hool bodied Volvo B10M T3 APT, formerly with Armchair, Brentford and B M Coaches, Hounslow before being purchased in March 2009.

The regular bus on the Maclennan Coaches school contract from the Nicolson Institute to Tolsta is Irizar Century bodied Scania K340EB4 PC09SFC, seen at the end of the run in Tolsta heading to the driver's home in Back. This vehicle was new to Princess Coaches in Southampton in May 2009 and was also registered 991 FOT and FT09 LCT. The vehicle joined the Maclennan Coaches fleet in March 2019. (Steven Macaskill)

Irizar i6 bodied Scania K340IB4 YP12 NUJ was new to Redwing Reliance, London and sold to Hebridean Transport in October 2019. Alongside it is similar Irizar i6 bodied Scania K340IB4 YP12 NUU. Both are parked up in Stornoway at the rear of Engebret Ltd petrol station on Sandwick Road.

New to Allan of Gorebridge as B17 DWA was Irizar Scania K114EB4 bodied SK54 BPY, which was also operated with Graham Urquhart of Inverness and Gibson Direct of Renfrew before being acquired by Maclennan Coaches. It is pictured awaiting cruise ship passengers for an island excursion.

Another view of Van Hool Alizee bodied Scania K114 SX04 XAC. Many vehicles are parked overnight at, or close to, their driver's homes.

Performing a school contract is Van Hool Alizee bodied Scania K114 SX04 XAC.

Jonkheere Mistral bodied Volvo B12M MJZ 3685 – new to Parks of Hamilton as SJ04 KFA (LSK 876). It was pictured at Bragar Primary School.

In the garage at Inaclete Road, Stornoway is Jonkheere bodied Volvo B12M FCZ 707, bought in March 2015, ex-Brogan of Ballmoney and McDermott of Portaferry (FN04 JZH).

Covering for the regular bus on the Tolsta run from the Nicolson Institute is Plaxton Panther bodied Volvo B9R YY14AFF. It is pictured having finished the service in North Tolsta. Originally new to Seaward Travel, Wembley, this vehicle passed to Maclennan in October 2019. (Steven Macaskill)

Plaxton Panther Paramount bodied Volvo B8R YX17 OHP was new to SMS, Towcester in March 2017 and acquired by Maclennan Coaches in October 2019.

Representing the smaller buses operated by the company is Mercedes-Benz O814D YN53 VBP.

A shot of similar Plaxton Cheetah Mercedes-Benz O816D YN59 BMZ passing by Stornoway Harbour. There are quite a few directional signposts beside it for tourists.

South Harris Coaches

Ford Transit AY16 YKD seen on a rare occasion in Stornoway. The company has routes covering local areas from the ferry terminal in Leverburgh.

Similar Ford Transit SY14 KAK seen in Marybank on the outskirts of Stornoway. (Donald Macarthur)

Peter Maclennan

Peter Maclennan operates a service from Stornoway to Timsgarry. LDV Convoy minibus YX07 EEY is seen here in Stornoway at the back of Engebret Ltd petrol station on Sandwick Road.

KVC bodied Mercedes-Benz 515CDI YN09 HDX seen at Stornoway ferry terminal about to operate a cruise ship tour.

One of the many Ford Transits operated by the company is YS63 VPF, which is seen on Shell Street in Stornoway. This vehicle later passed to Maclennan Coaches.

EVM Grand Tourer bodied Mercedes-Benz 516 Cdi Sprinter was new as RK68 GVO, replacing Iveco Daily RK69 ZPJ, which the company found unsuitable.

EVM Grand Tourer bodied Mercedes-Benz 516 Cdi Sprinter in Stornoway bus station.

Mercedes-Benz Vito SF69 WOD, bought new in October 2019, is pictured at the ex-RAF site in Aird Uig after completing the feeder service from Timsgarry. (Donald Macarthur)

Other Operators

Hebridean Minibus Service operate a feeder service to Dell, Cross, Eorodale and Skigersta in Ness which connects with the Lochs Motor Transport service to Stornoway. Pictured is UVM bodied Mercedes-Benz 413CDi LX53 EXO. This vehicle is now being used as a mobile shop in South Harris.

Up until 2016, Royal Mail operated four Postbus services on the Western Isles capable of carrying up to four passengers. These were withdrawn due to dwindling passenger numbers and replaced by larger delivery vans able to carry more parcels. LDV Convoy minibus BX58 UMG was pictured in 2010 on a service from Stornoway bus station to Timsgarry.

Plaxton Paramount Volvo B10M A5 EXR in Tarbert. It was new to Ambassador Travel as H172 EJU in April 1991. It also served with Kings Ferry, Gillingham as H282 NRF. (Donald Macarthur)

EVM bodied Mercedes 515Cdi RJ60 UHN was new to Scalpay Minibus Committee and used on the service from Tarbert to Scalpay until October 2019.

Uig Bus Services Ford Transit BG52 VJU seen at Stornoway ferry terminal. This was used on the Uig feeder services from Garynahine.

Iveco bodied SF06 BFE seen at Stornoway bus station. This vehicle was operated by Staran/Third Sector Hebrides on the evening services to the North Lochs area. It was acquired from Mobus of Leven.

Visiting Vehicles to the Western Isles

VTV169S is an Eastern Coachworks bodied Bristol VRT which was new to East Midland. It has been converted and is now used as a Community Outreach vehicle by People With A Mission Ministries (PWAMM), based in Perth. This vehicle was based in Lewis for a few years and is seen in Tong alongside Bus na Comhairle's BMC 1100FE B135 (YJ05KOW). (Donald Macarthur)

A regular visitor to the island was mobile evangelical centre Challenger 4 Neoplan Skyliner N122/3 IUI 2129, which was originally new to Durham Travel Service. It toured various churches around the villages. (Donald Macarthur)

Outside the Town Hall in Stornoway, East Lancs Dennis Trident 200 XJJ acts as a mobile exhibition promoting stays in Scotland.

East Lancs Dennis Trident 200 XJJ has appeared in various guises with different operators. It visited the Western Isles in 2010 promoting Visit Scotland.

Preserved Buses on the Western Isles

By far the oldest vehicle on the Western Isles is a very smart 1924 Model T Ford (JS 1972) that was discovered in East Sussex and lovingly restored.

As mentioned in the foreword, the Western Isles Transport Preservation Group (WITPG) has acquired an old fish farm processing plant at Marybank Industrial Estate near Stornoway. It is being used as a base for their operations they are trying to generate funding to renovate the building for use as a future museum site. There are sheds in various parts of Lewis that house old coaches in various stages of preservation. Plaxton-bodied B294 KPF, in the livery of Galson Motors, started life with London Country Buses Greenline as TPL 94.

Printed and bound by CPI Group (UK) Ltd, Croydon, CR0 4YY

20/03/2026

02075431-0001